FERTILITY COOKBOOK

40+ Muffins, Pancakes and Cookie recipes for a healthy and balanced Fertility diet

TABLE OF CONTENTS

Introduction

Fertility recipes for personal enjoyment but also for family enjoyment You will love them for sure for how easy it is to prepare them.

BREAKFAST

CINNAMON QUINOA BREAKFAST

Serves: **4**

Prep Time: **10**   Minutes

Cook Time: **20**   Minutes

Total Time: **30**   Minutes

INGREDIENTS

- ½ cup quinoa
- 1 cup almond milk
- 1 cinnamon sticks
- pinch of salt
- toasted almonds
- toasted coconut flakes
- blueberries

DIRECTIONS

1. In a saucepan add almond milk, salt, cinnamon sticks and bring to a simmer for 15-18 minutes
2. Remove from heat and let it stand for 5-6 minutes
3. Scoop half of the quinoa into a bowl and serve with toppings

WAFFLES

Serves: **6**

Prep Time: **10** Minutes

Cook Time: **10** Minutes

Total Time: **20** Minutes

INGREDIENTS

- 2 cups flour
- 2 tsp baking powder
- ¼ tsp baking soda
- ½ tsp salt
- 2 egg
- 2 cups vanilla soy yogurt
- 1 tablespoons coconut oil

DIRECTIONS

1. In a bowl mix all dry ingredients together and let the mixture sit for a couple of minutes
2. In another bowl mix remaining ingredients and and combine both mixtures
3. Cook on preheated griddle and serve with sautéed apples and maple syrup

BERRY MATCHA

Serves: *4*

Prep Time: *10* Minutes

Cook Time: *10* Minutes

Total Time: *20* Minutes

INGREDIENTS

- ¼ cup orange juice
- 1 tsp matcha
- 1 tsp water
- ½ cup strawberries
- ½ cup blueberries
- ¼ banana

DIRECTIONS

1. In a bowl matcha, water, strawberries and banana
2. In a blender all add ingredients and blend until smooth
3. Pour into a glass and serve

GLUTEN FREE MUESLI SCONE

Serves: **12**

Prep Time: **10**   Minutes

Cook Time: **20**   Minutes

Total Time: **30**   Minutes

INGREDIENTS

- 2 cups almond flour
- ¼ tsp salt
- ¼ tsp baking soda
- ½ cup dried cranberries
- ½ cup apricots
- ½ cup sunflower seeds
- ½ cup sesame seeds
- 1 tablespoon agave nectar
- 1 egg

DIRECTIONS

1. Preheat the oven to 325 F
2. In a bowl mix flour, soda and salt
3. Stir in nuts, seeds, dried fruit, agave and egg
4. Mix well until dough is formed and cut into 12-14 squares
5. Place on a lined baking sheet and bake for 12-15 minutes

NUT BARS

Serves: **8**

Prep Time: **5** Minutes

Cook Time: **5** Minutes

Total Time: **10** Minutes

INGREDIENTS

- 1 cup unsweetened coconut
- 1 cup dried cranberries
- 1 cup unsalted cashews
- ¼ tsp salt
- 1 tablespoon honey
- 1 tablespoon coconut oil
- ¼ tsp cinnamon

DIRECTIONS

1. In a blender add all ingredients except honey and cashews and blend until smooth
2. When ready add cashews and honey and spoon mixture onto a wax paper
3. Refrigerate for 2-3 hours, cut into bars and serve

AVOCADO TOAST

Serves: **4**

Prep Time: **10**   Minutes

Cook Time: **10**   Minutes

Total Time: **20**   Minutes

INGREDIENTS

- 2 ripe avocados
- 3 oz. feta
- 2 tablespoons mint
- ½ lemon
- 3 slices grain bread

DIRECTIONS

1. Place avocado in a bowl and mash, add mint, lemon juice and mix well
2. Season with black pepper, salt and toast bread whole wheat bread until golden
3. Spoon ¼ of the avocado mixture onto each slice of bread
4. Top with feta and serve

Serves: 2

Prep Time: *10*   Minutes

Cook Time: *30*   Minutes

Total Time: *40*   Minutes

INGREDIENTS

- ½ cup unsalted cashews
- ¼ cup coconut water
- ¾ cup coconut meat
- 1 tsp vanilla
- drizzle of maple syrup
- 1 tablespoon blueberries
- 1 tablespoon gluten free granola

DIRECTIONS

1. In a bowl soak cashew for 15-20 minutes
2. Cut out the inner meat of the coconut
3. Pour cashews, coconut meat, coconut water, vanilla and blend until smooth
4. Pour into a bowl and top with blueberries and serve

MUSHROOM OMELETTE

Serves: *1*

Prep Time: 5   Minutes

Cook Time: *10* Minutes

Total Time: *15* Minutes

INGREDIENTS

- 2 eggs
- ¼ tsp salt
- ¼ tsp black pepper
- 1 tablespoon olive oil
- ¼ cup cheese
- ¼ tsp basil
- 1 cup mushrooms

DIRECTIONS

1. In a bowl combine all ingredients together and mix well
2. In a skillet heat olive oil and pour the egg mixture
3. Cook for 1-2 minutes per side
4. When ready remove omelette from the skillet and serve

"GOOD MORNING" BROWNIES

Serves: **10**

Prep Time: **5**   Minutes

Cook Time: **15**   Minutes

Total Time: **20**   Minutes

INGREDIENTS

- 15 oz black beans
- 1/3 cup oats
- 1/3 tsp salt
- 1 ½ tbs sugar
- ½ cup maple syrup
- 2 ½ tbs cocoa powder
- 3 tbs vanilla
- 1 tsp baking powder
- 1 cup chocolate chips
- 1/3 cup coconut oil

DIRECTIONS

1. Preheat the oven to 375F
2. Blend all ingredients together except chocolate chips
3. Fold in the chocolate chips and pour the batter into a greased pan
4. Cook for at least 15 minutes, allow to cool and then serve

BANANA OATMEAL

Serves: *4*

Prep Time: *10*   Minutes

Cook Time: *8*   Hours

Total Time: *8*   Hours

INGREDIENTS

- 1 cup oats
- 1/3 tsp salt
- 3 tbs almond butter
- 3 cups water
- 2 bananas
- 2 tbs honey
- 1 ½ cups milk

DIRECTIONS

1. Mix water, milk, salt and oats and place in a slow cooker
2. Cook covered for about 8 hours
3. Place into bowls, add almond butter and honey and top with banana slices
4. Serve

CHINESE OMELET

Serves: **1**

Prep Time: **5** Minutes

Cook Time: **5** Minutes

Total Time: **10** Minutes

INGREDIENTS

- 2 eggs
- 1/3 cup tomato
- 1/3 cup kale
- 1/3 cup green onion
- 1 ½ tbs sour cream
- 2 tsp garlic

DIRECTIONS

1. Whisk the eggs and sour cream together until light
2. Saute the chopped vegetables for about 3 minutes
3. Pour in the eggs and cook until done
4. Serve immediately

BLUEBERRIES OATMEAL

Serves: **2**

Prep Time: **10** Minutes

Cook Time: **8** Hours

Total Time: **8** Hours

INGREDIENTS

- 1/3 cup oats
- 1/3 cup blueberries
- 2 tbs maple syrup
- 1/3 cup coconut milk
- ½ tsp vanilla
- 1 banana
- 1 ½ tsp chia seeds

DIRECTIONS

1. Mix the oats and chia seeds together
2. Pour in the milk and top with blueberries and sliced banana
3. Refrigerate for at least 8 hours
4. Stir in the maple syrup and serve

CHIA PUDDING

Serves: 2

Prep Time: 5   Minutes

Cook Time: 10   Minutes

Total Time: 15   Minutes

INGREDIENTS

- 5 tbs chia seeds
- 1 ½ tbs vanilla
- 2 tbs maple syrup
- 2 ½ cup almond milk
- 1 ½ cup strawberries
- 1 beet

DIRECTIONS

1. Blend together the milk, strawberries, chopped beet, maple syrup, and vanilla
2. Pour into a cup and ad the chia
3. Stir every 5 minutes for 15 minutes
4. Refrigerate overnight
5. Serve topped with fruits

BREAKFAST CASSEROLE

Serves: *4*

Prep Time: *10*   Minutes

Cook Time: *35*   Minutes

Total Time: *45*   Minutes

INGREDIENTS

- 7 oz asparagus
- 3 tbs parsley
- 1 cup broccoli
- 1 zucchini
- 3 tbs oil
- 5 eggs
- Salt
- Pepper

DIRECTIONS

1. Cook the diced zucchini, asparagus and broccoli florets in heated oil for about 5 minutes
2. Season with salt and pepper and remove from heat
3. Whisk the eggs and season then add the parsley
4. Place the vegetables in a greased pan then pour the eggs over
5. Bake in the preheated oven for about 35 minutes at 350F

PANCAKES

BANANA PANCAKES

Serves: **4**

Prep Time: **10**   Minutes

Cook Time: **20**   Minutes

Total Time: **30**   Minutes

INGREDIENTS

- 1 cup whole wheat flour
- ¼ tsp baking soda
- ¼ tsp baking powder
- 1 cup mashed banana
- 2 eggs
- 1 cup milk

DIRECTIONS

1. In a bowl combine all ingredients together and mix well
2. In a skillet heat olive oil
3. Pour ¼ of the batter and cook each pancake for 1-2 minutes per side
4. When ready remove from heat and serve

QUINOA PANCAKES

Serves: **2**

Prep Time: **10**   Minutes

Cook Time: **10**   Minutes

Total Time: **20**   Minutes

INGREDIENTS

- 1 cup almond flour
- ¼ cup cooked quinoa
- 2 tsp baking soda
- pinch of salt
- 1 tsp cinnamon
- 1 cup almond milk
- 1 tablespoon flax meal
- 1 tablespoon agave

DIRECTIONS

1. In a bowl add baking soda, cinnamon, almond flour, quinoa, salt and mix well
2. Whisk together flax meal, water, agave and almond milk
3. In a bowl mix dry ingredients and wet ingredients
4. In a skillet add batter and cook for 1-2 minutes per side
5. When ready, remove and serve

GLUTEN FREE PANCAKES

Serves: **6**

Prep Time: **10**   Minutes

Cook Time: **10**   Minutes

Total Time: **20**   Minutes

INGREDIENTS

- 2 cups almond flour
- ¼ cup coconut cream
- 6 eggs
- ¼ cup melted butter
- ½ cup agave nectar
- 1 tablespoon vanilla extract
- 1 tsp baking soda
- 1 pinch salt

DIRECTIONS

1. In a blender add all ingredients and blend until smooth
2. Melt butter in a skillet and pour 1-2 tablespoons of batter
3. Cook for 2-3 minutes per side, remove and serve

HEALHTY JELLO – NO SUGAR ADDED

Serves: **4**

Prep Time: **5**   Minutes

Cook Time: **5**   Minutes

Total Time: **10** Minutes

INGREDIENTS

- ½ cup water
- ½ cup water
- 1 tablespoon gelatin
- 1 cup no sugar organic juice

DIRECTIONS

1. Stir gelatin in water and mix well
2. Stir in juice and mix well
3. Pour into a container and refrigerate overnight

SUGAR-FREE STRAWBERRY GUMMIES

Serves: **20**

Prep Time: **10**   Minutes

Cook Time: **10**   Minutes

Total Time: **20**   Minutes

INGREDIENTS

- 1 cup strawberries
- ¾ cup water
- 2 tablespoons gelatin
- 1 tablespoon maple syrup

DIRECTIONS

1. In a pan add water and berries and cook right under boiling, then remove from heat
2. Place mixture in blender and mix well
3. Add gelatin and blend again
4. Pour into silicone molds and refrigerate for a couple of hours, remove and serve

TURMERIC CHIA PUDDING

Serves: **1**

Prep Time: **10** Minutes

Cook Time: **60** Minutes

Total Time: **70** Minutes

INGREDIENTS

- 1 cup coconut milk
- 1 scoop collagen peptides
- 1 tablespoon chia seeds
- dash of cinnamon
- 1 scoop turmeric tonic
- toppings (unsweetened flaked coconut)

DIRECTIONS

1. In a bowl mix all ingredients and place in a bowl
2. Refrigerate for 60 minutes
3. Remove and top with preferred favorite toppings

CHOCOLATE FUDGE

Serves: **12**

Prep Time: **10** Minutes

Cook Time: **10** Minutes

Total Time: **20** Minutes

INGREDIENTS

- ½ cup cashew butter
- 1 tablespoon maple ghee
- 1 tablespoon cacao powder
- pinch of salt
- 2 tablespoons sugar-free sweetener
- ½ cup dark chocolate chips
- ½ cup melted coconut butter
- ½ cup collagen peptides
- ½ tsp peppermint extract
- 1 tablespoon MCT oil

DIRECTIONS

1. In a bowl add all ingredients and microwave until fully melted
2. Pour into a pan with parchment paper and chill, refrigerate before serving

APPLE CINNAMON DESSERT

Serves: **4**

Prep Time: **10** Minutes

Cook Time: **20** Minutes

Total Time: **30** Minutes

INGREDIENTS

- 2 chopped apples
- 1 tablespoon butter
- ¼ tsp cinnamon
- 2 tsp lemon juice
- 2 tablespoons honey

DIRECTIONS

1. Preheat the oven to 350 F
2. In a bowl mix all ingredients together
3. Bake for 15-18 minutes or until golden brown
4. Remove and serve

BREAKFAST COOKIES

Serves: *8-12*

Prep Time: *5*   Minutes

Cook Time: *15*   Minutes

Total Time: *20*   Minutes

INGREDIENTS

- 1 cup rolled oats
- ¼ cup applesauce
- ½ tsp vanilla extract
- 3 tablespoons chocolate chips
- 2 tablespoons dried fruits
- 1 tsp cinnamon

DIRECTIONS

1. Preheat the oven to 325 F
2. In a bowl combine all ingredients together and mix well
3. Scoop cookies using an ice cream scoop
4. Place cookies onto a prepared baking sheet
5. Place in the oven for 12-15 minutes or until the cookies are done
6. When ready remove from the oven and serve

BREAKFAST COOKIES

Serves: **15**

Prep Time: **10** Minutes

Cook Time: **40** Minutes

Total Time: **50** Minutes

INGREDIENTS

- 1 cup oats
- 2 tsp vanilla
- 1/3 cup honey
- ¼ tsp salt
- 2 ½ tbs coconut oil
- 1 egg
- 1 cup apple
- 1 cup flour
- 2 tsp baking powder
- 2 tsp cinnamon

DIRECTIONS

1. Mix the flour, oats, cinnamon, baking powder, and salt together
2. Mix the coconut butter, egg and vanilla well, then add the honey
3. Mix the wet and dry ingredients together then add the diced apple
4. Refrigerate for at least 30 minutes

28

5. Divide the dough into 15 scoops on a lined baking sheet
6. Bake in the preheated oven for about 15 minutes at 320F
7. Allow to cool the serve

CHINESE ALMOND COOKIES

Serves: **6**

Prep Time: **10**   Minutes

Cook Time: **25**   Minutes

Total Time: **35**   Minutes

INGREDIENTS

- 2 cups flour
- ½ tsp salt
- 1 cup sugar
- 1 egg
- ½ cup almonds
- ½ tsp soda
- 1 tsp almond extract

DIRECTIONS

1. In a bowl sift sugar, soda, salt and flour
2. Add egg, almond extract and mix well
3. Shape dough into 1-inch balls and place on a cookie sheet
4. Bake at 300 F for 20 minutes
5. Remove and serve

SNACKS & DRINKS

AVOCADO BLUEBERRY SMOOTHIE

Serves: **1**

Prep Time: **5** Minutes

Cook Time: **5** Minutes

Total Time: **10** Minutes

INGREDIENTS

- 1 cup blueberries
- 1 cup frozen mango
- ½ avocado
- 1 tablespoon chia seeds
- 1 tsp Maca powder2
- 1 tablespoon honey

DIRECTIONS

1. In a blender place all ingredients and blend until smooth
2. Pour smoothie in a glass and serve

Serves: **1**

Prep Time: **5** Minutes

Cook Time: **5** Minutes

Total Time: **10** Minutes

INGREDIENTS

- 1 cup blueberries
- ½ cup strawberries
- ½ banana
- ½ avocado
- 1 tsp hemp seeds

DIRECTIONS

1. In a blender place all ingredients and blend until smooth
2. Pour smoothie in a glass and serve

BEERY SMOOTHIE

Serves: **1**

Prep Time: **5**   Minutes

Cook Time: **5**   Minutes

Total Time: **10** Minutes

INGREDIENTS

- ½ cup cranberry juice
- 2/3 cup silken tofu
- ½ cup raspberries
- ¼ cup blueberries

DIRECTIONS

1. In a blender place all ingredients and blend until smooth
2. Pour smoothie in a glass and serve

BANANA SMOOTHIE

Serves: *1*

Prep Time: *5*   Minutes

Cook Time: *5*   Minutes

Total Time: *10*   Minutes

INGREDIENTS

- 1 banana
- ½ cup almond
- 1 tablespoon honey
- 1 tablespoon oat

DIRECTIONS

1. In a blender place all ingredients and blend until smooth
2. Pour smoothie in a glass and serve

APPLE SMOOTHIE

Serves: **1**

Prep Time: **5**   Minutes

Cook Time: **5**   Minutes

Total Time: **10** Minutes

INGREDIENTS

- 1 apple
- ½ cup applesauce
- ½ cup almond
- 1 tablespoon honey
- 1 tablespoon oat

DIRECTIONS

1. In a blender place all ingredients and blend until smooth
2. Pour smoothie in a glass and serve

MANGO SMOOTHIE

Serves: **1**

Prep Time: **5**   Minutes

Cook Time: **5**   Minutes

Total Time: **10** Minutes

INGREDIENTS

- 1 manco
- ½ cup almond
- 1 tablespoon honey
- 1 tablespoon oats

DIRECTIONS

1. In a blender place all ingredients and blend until smooth
2. Pour smoothie in a glass and serve

STRAWBERRY SMOOTHIE

Serves: *1*

Prep Time: *5*   Minutes

Cook Time: *5*   Minutes

Total Time: *10* Minutes

INGREDIENTS

- ¾ cup strawberries
- ½ cup liquid pasteurized egg whites
- ½ cup ice
- 1 tablespoon sugar

DIRECTIONS

1. In a blender place all ingredients and blend until smooth
2. Pour smoothie in a glass and serve

PEACH SMOOTHIE

Serves: **1**

Prep Time: **5**   Minutes

Cook Time: **5**   Minutes

Total Time: **10**   Minutes

INGREDIENTS

- ½ cup ice
- 2 tablespoons powdered egg whites
- ¾ peaches
- 1 tablespoon sugar

DIRECTIONS

1. In a blender place all ingredients and blend until smooth
2. Pour smoothie in a glass and serve

FRUITY SHAKE

Serves: **1**

Prep Time: **5** Minutes

Cook Time: **5** Minutes

Total Time: **10** Minutes

INGREDIENTS

- 6 oz. fruit cocktail
- 2 scoops protein powder
- 1 cup water
- ice cubes

DIRECTIONS

1. In a blender place all ingredients and blend until smooth
2. Pour smoothie in a glass and serve

MUFFINS

BLUEBERRY MUFFINS

Serves: **6**

Prep Time: **10**   Minutes

Cook Time: **20**   Minutes

Total Time: **30**   Minutes

INGREDIENTS

- ½ cup coconut flour
- ¼ tsp salt
- ¼ tsp baking soda
- 5 eggs
- 1 cup agave nectar
- 1 tablespoon vanilla extract
- 1 cup blueberries

DIRECTIONS

1. Preheat the oven to 325 F
2. In a bowl mix all muffins
3. Fold in blueberries
4. Place batter into a muffin pan and bake at 20-25 minutes
5. Remove and serve

BANANA WALNUT MUFFINS

Serves: **8**

Prep Time: **10**   Minutes

Cook Time: **20**   Minutes

Total Time: **30**   Minutes

INGREDIENTS

- 2 eggs
- ½ cup coconut oil
- 2 bananas
- 2 dates
- 8 drops stevia
- ¼ cup coconut flour
- ½ tsp salt
- ¼ tsp baking soda
- ¼ cup walnuts

DIRECTIONS

1. In a blender add oil, bananas, eggs, stevia, dates and blend until smooth
2. Add in baking soda, coconut flour, salt and blend again
3. Fold walnuts into batter and scoop ¼ cup into a muffin pan
4. Bake for 20 minutes or until golden brown
5. When ready, remove and serve

SIMPLE MUFFINS

Serves: *8-12*

Prep Time: *10*   Minutes

Cook Time: *20*   Minutes

Total Time: *30*   Minutes

INGREDIENTS

- 2 eggs
- 1 tablespoon olive oil
- 1 cup milk
- 2 cups whole wheat flour
- 1 tsp baking soda
- ¼ tsp baking soda
- 1 cup pumpkin puree
- 1 tsp cinnamon
- ¼ cup molasses

DIRECTIONS

1. In a bowl combine all wet ingredients
2. In another bowl combine all dry ingredients
3. Combine wet and dry ingredients together
4. Pour mixture into 8-12 prepared muffin cups, fill 2/3 of the cups
5. Bake for 18-20 minutes at 375 F, when ready remove and serve

CARROT MUFFIN

Serves: *8*

Prep Time: *10*   Minutes

Cook Time: *25*   Minutes

Total Time: *35*   Minutes

INGREDIENTS

- 2 cups almond flour
- 2 tsp baking soda
- 1 tsp salt
- 1 tablespoon cinnamon
- 1 cup dates
- 2 bananas
- 2 eggs
- 1 tsp apple cider vinegar
- ½ cup coconut oil
- 1 cup carrots
- ¾ cup walnuts

DIRECTIONS

1. Preheat the oven to 325 F
2. In a bowl mix baking soda, salt, almond flour and cinnamon
3. In a blender add vinegar, oil, eggs, dates, bananas and blend until smooth

4. Transfer mixture to a bowl and mix with dry mixture
5. Fold in carrots walnuts and spoon mixture into muffin pans
6. Bake for 20-25 minutes, remove and serve

BRAN MUFFINS

Serves: *8*

Prep Time: *10*   Minutes

Cook Time: *25*   Minutes

Total Time: *35*   Minutes

INGREDIENTS

- ½ cup almond flour
- ¼ cup flaxseed meal
- 1 tsp baking soda
- 5 dates
- 2 eggs
- 2 tablespoons olive oil
- ½ cup water
- ½ cup sesame seeds
- ½ cup sunflower seeds
- ¼ cup raisins

DIRECTIONS

1. Preheat the oven to 325 F
2. In a bowl mix all ingredients
3. Place in a blender and blend until smooth
4. Spoon batter into a muffin pan

5. Bake for 25 minutes, remove and serve

LEMON MUFFINS

Serves: *8*

Prep Time: *10*   Minutes

Cook Time: *15*   Minutes

Total Time: *25*   Minutes

INGREDIENTS

- ½ cup coconut flour
- ½ tsp salt
- ½ tsp baking soda
- 2 eggs
- ½ cup agave nectar
- ½ cup oil
- 1 tablespoon lemon zest
- 1 tablespoon poppy seeds

DIRECTIONS

1. In a bowl mix all ingredients together
2. Blend dry ingredients into wet, fold in poppy seeds
3. Spoon batter into each muffin cup and bake for 12-15 minutes
4. Remove and serve

ALMOND MUFFINS

Serves: *8*

Prep Time: *10*   Minutes

Cook Time: *15*   Minutes

Total Time: *25*   Minutes

INGREDIENTS

- 1 cup almond flour
- 2 eggs
- 1 tablespoon agave nectar
- ½ tsp baking soda
- ¼ tsp apple cider vinegar

DIRECTIONS

1. Preheat the oven at 325 F
2. In a bowl mix baking soda, almond flour, eggs, vinegar and agave
3. Scoop batter into muffin pans and bake for 12-15 minutes
4. Remove and serve with raspberry spread

THANK YOU FOR READING THIS BOOK!

CPSIA information can be obtained
at www.ICGtesting.com
Printed in the USA
BVHW031135240321
603178BV00020B/60

9 781664 063037